THESE LANDS ARE OURS

TECUMSEH'S FIGHT FOR THE OLD NORTHWEST

BY KATE CONNELL

ALEX HALEY, GENERAL EDITOR

ILLUSTRATIONS BY
JAN NAIMO JONES

RSVP
RAINTREE
STECK-VAUGHN
PUBLISHERS
The Steck-Vaughn Company

Austin, Texas

Published by Steck-Vaughn Company.

Text, illustrations, and cover art copyright © 1993 by Dialogue Systems Inc., 627 Broadway, New York, New York 10012. All rights reserved.

Cover art by John Edens. The cover portrait is based on two famous portraits of Tecumseh, neither of which he sat for. One was a sketch done by Pierre Le Dru in which Tecumseh is shown in a uniform like the one on the cover. The other was a painting done by an unknown artist. Both portraits are thought to be acceptable likenesses. Both show him in non-Shawnee dress, though some consider it unlikely that he would have been so attired.

Printed in the United States of America
1 2 3 4 5 6 7 8 9   R   98 97 96 95 94 93 92

Library of Congress Cataloging-in-Publication Data

Connell, Kate, 1954–
    These lands are ours: Tecumseh's fight for the old
northwest / by Kate Connell; illustrator, Jan N. Jones.
        p.   cm.—(Stories of America)
    Summary: Discusses the life of the Shawnee warrior,
orator, and leader who united a confederacy of Indians in an
effort to save Indian land from the advance of white soldiers
and settlers.
    ISBN 0-8114-7227-2.—ISBN 0-8114-8067-4 (pbk.)
    1. Tecumseh, Shawnee Chief, 1768–1813—Juvenile litera-
ture.   2. Shawnee Indians—Biography—Juvenile literature.
3. Shawnee Indians—History—Juvenile literature.   4. Indians of North America—Wars—1812–1815—Juvenile literature.
5. Northwest, Old—History—1775–1865—Juvenile literature.   [1. Tecumseh, Shawnee Chief, 1768–1813.   2. Shawnee Indians—Biography.   3. Indians of North America—
Biography.]   I. Jones, Jan N., ill.   II. Title.   III. Series.
E99.S35T1155 1993
977′.00497302—dc20
[B]   92-14417
                                                           CIP
                                                            AC

ISBN 0-8114-7227-2 (Hardcover)
ISBN 0-8114-8067-4 (Softcover)

Introduction

by Alex Haley, General Editor

Part of my childhood was spent playing "Cowboys and Indians," a game of make-believe based on the movies we watched. We would chase each other around whooping and yelling, firing cap pistols or pointed fingers as we yelled "Bang! You're dead. Bang! Got you!" ("No you didn't," was always the reply.) The Indians were never "us." They were either invisible, ghosts of our imaginations, or little kids dragged into the game because we were bigger. No one wanted to be an Indian, everyone wanted to the hero. That was what we knew then. We knew the movies, not the history.

The war between the American Indian peoples and the white newcomers was longer by far than any other war in our history. It began soon after Jamestown was founded in 1607 and lasted almost into this century. Name it in terms of its length and it could be called "The Three Hundred Years War." Think of it in terms of a people defending their land, homes, and families against terrible odds, and you will discover something else. You will discover many new heroes. Not surprisingly, many of them—like the Apache Geronimo, the Oglala Sioux Crazy Horse, the Seminole Osceola, the Ottawa Pontiac, and the Wampanoag Metacom—were warriors. Others, like the Nez Perce Chief Joseph and the Cherokee Sequoyah, were statesmen. And some, like the Shawnee Tecumseh—the subject of this book—were both.

Contents

▲▲▲

Prologue

May 30, 1779

It was not yet dawn. The Shawnee village of Chillicothe slept. Inside their wigwams people lay curled on blankets, lulled by the peaceful sound of flowing water from the Little Miami River. A few birds twittered faintly, early risers on this May morning.

But not the earliest. A few hundred yards away, a lone Shawnee hunter was up and awake, returning to the village after his hunt. Riding through the prairie grass, he stopped abruptly. Something had caught his eye. He looked closer and then, with a hard kick at his horse, took off at a gallop toward the village. Crouched low over the neck of his horse, he shouted a warning—Long Knives!—but it was too late. A man's form rose up out of the grass, took aim with a rifle, and fired. The hunter tumbled from his horse. The man ran to where he

lay and drew out a long hunting knife. With one deft stroke, the Shawnee's scalp was his.

The man tucked the bloody scalp into his belt and looked around. All was quiet. Several other shadowy figures rose up out of the grass. They motioned cautiously to one another and, with rifles at the ready, began moving toward Chillicothe.

▲ ▲ ▲

In the village, a noise wrenched Black Fish from his sleep. A gunshot and, he thought, yelling. The chief knew instantly what was happening. He seized his rifle and burst from the wigwam. Long Knives! he shouted. Long Knives!! Get to the woods!

The village came alive. As women and children scrambled for safety, Black Fish quickly rallied his warriors. He led them at a run in the direction of the shot. Spotting the line of white frontiersmen coming through the grass, the Shawnees dropped to their knees and started shooting.

Black Fish and his men were vastly outnumbered—there were 265 Kentucky frontiersmen to his 25 Shawnees—but they managed to hold the Kentuckians back long enough for some of the women and children to flee to the woods. The rest retreated to the stout log council house. Finally, under a hail of bullets, Black Fish's warriors also fell back to the council house.

They came in breathlessly, carrying a body with them. It was Black Fish. He'd been shot. They laid him down as gently as they could. Covered with blood, struggling to breathe, he ordered his warriors to fight to the death.

And so they fought off the Long Knives from inside the council house. They fired through chinks in the walls—twenty-five warriors and about fifteen boys who could shoot. The women and small children kept up a chorus of defiant screams and war whoops. The ancient village medicine man chanted prayers to the Great Spirit to help the warriors in their task.

Outside the council house, the Kentuckians began to get fed up. Nothing would penetrate those hickory log walls, they decided, except cannon, and they didn't have cannon. So at a signal from their commander they split up. Some kept shooting at the council house, to keep the Shawnees inside busy. The rest started ransacking the village. In and out of the empty wigwams they went, laughing and cursing, taking blankets, tools, clothes, silver jewelry—anything of value. They stole the Shawnees' horses that were tied up on the plain. They stole as much as they could carry and then set the wigwams on fire.

In the middle of all this madness, the Kentuckians came across an old black woman, a former slave living in the village. She told them that a hundred warriors were on the way. Word spread like wildfire. In the confusion the number of approaching warriors grew to five hundred. Finally the Kentuckians fled in a panic, carrying their loot through the woods.

With wild war cries, the Shawnee men and boys set off after them. They chased them for twenty miles, shooting as they went. In all, three Shawnees and eleven Kentuckians were killed that day. A week later, Black Fish died of his wounds.

▲ ▲ ▲

Black Fish had an adopted eleven-year-old son in the village, a boy whose father had been killed in battle by Long Knives. The boy was exceptional, so everyone said. He was bright

5 ◭

and energetic and could already shoot almost as well as a man. He was almost certainly in the council house that day, firing back at the Long Knives for all he was worth. The boy's name was Tecumseh.

Tecumseh was not a warrior—yet. He was only eleven. But he knew about war. He knew that war had taken his father when he was six years old. Now Black Fish, too, was dead.

He knew that war had driven his mother away. She had taken his little sister and migrated west with a thousand other Shawnees to get away from the killing and burning. He never saw her again.

He also knew that war must go on, because the Long Knives were greedy—greedy for land. They would drive his people right off their hunting grounds if they didn't fight back.

Tecumseh was not yet a warrior, but he had already chosen the warrior's path. This story is about how he walked that path to the end.

1 A Man of Note

It was a fresh spring afternoon in 1807, and just about everyone in the Shawnee village at Greenville, Ohio, was outdoors. Some women were farming corn near the creek, while others stirred steaming cook pots in the village. Most of the men were in the woods, felling saplings for new wigwams. Everywhere, children were underfoot.

Inside one wigwam, though, a group of men sat in a tight circle, talking in low voices. A shaft of bright sunlight fell through the doorway, lighting up their faces. They were all dressed alike, in simple warrior's buckskins, but one was clearly the leader. When he spoke, the others listened. When he flashed his white teeth in a smile, they smiled, too. They were devoted to him. He was their chief, Tecumseh.

Not quite forty years old, Tecumseh was now a man in the prime of life. He had grown from an athletic boy into a powerful, muscular man. He had changed in some ways. His face had hardened, and when he got angry, his temper could be volcanic. But he still had the same clear hazel eyes, the same grave expression. A keen intelligence shone from those eyes, and a dignity that kept him from losing his temper very often. His shock of black hair was now adorned with a single eagle feather, the mark of a chief.

Today, in his circle of close friends, Tecumseh was neither angry nor particularly dignified. He was laughing when a young brave entered the wigwam.

Anthony Shane is here, he told Tecumseh. He brings a message. Would Tecumseh see him?

Of course he would. Tecumseh had known Shane since they were boys together in Chillicothe. Shane's father was a white trader, but his mother was a Shawnee. Tecumseh, who knew that Shane sometimes worked for the white government agent at Fort Wayne, immediately

▲ 8

wondered what the message was about. It couldn't be anything good, not if it came from Fort Wayne. But he kept his thoughts to himself as he welcomed Shane into the wigwam. The others made room for him, and Shane sat down in their circle.

Shane was wary as he greeted Tecumseh. He had indeed come on behalf of the white agent at Fort Wayne, whose name was William Wells. Wells had received a letter from none other than President Jefferson. Part of it was addressed to Tecumseh and his younger brother, a holy man known as the Prophet. Wells had sent Shane to tell the Shawnee brothers to come to Fort Wayne so he could read the letter to them.

But Shane knew they wouldn't go. Oh, the Prophet might—he loved to feel important. But Tecumseh never would, and he wouldn't let his brother go either. Tecumseh despised Wells.

The redheaded Wells had been an Indian once. As a teenager he was captured by the Miamis. Apekonit they called him—Wild Carrot—because of his hair. For eight years Apekonit lived as one of them. He'd grown into a fierce young brave, and when the Miamis and Shawnees joined forces against the Long Knives, he had fought hard alongside his brother warriors.

But after a string of Indian victories, Apekonit had switched sides. Now he worked for the government of the Long Knives.

What's more, Wells had lately been spreading rumors about the Prophet, trying to get him in trouble with the government. So when Shane told Tecumseh what Wells wanted, Tecumseh didn't even bother to consult his chiefs, who were sitting right there.

"Tell Captain Wells," he said without hesitation, "that my fire is kindled on the spot appointed by the Great Spirit. If he has anything to communicate to me, he must come here." In six days Tecumseh would call a great council to hear Wells speak. Wells should come then.

▲ ▲ ▲

Six days later, two hundred villagers were gathered in the vast council house at Greenville. They sat shoulder to shoulder around the fire, row upon row of them. Firelight gleamed on their bare arms and chests. Its reflection flickered in their eyes. A few men puffed on pipes, filling the air with pungent smoke. The din of their voices echoed from the rafters.

In front, closest to the fire, sat the head men and sachems.[1] Among them were the two village leaders, Tecumseh and the Prophet. The Prophet was six years younger than his brother, though he didn't look it. He was soft and fleshy and had only one good eye. He'd lost the other in an accident years before. His bulky figure was draped with the sacred necklaces and medicine bag of a holy man. As one who possessed supernatural powers, the Prophet commanded great respect. But it was a respect tinged with fear.

The flap of the council house door lifted and a man entered. Hundreds of gleaming eyes fastened on this lone figure. For a moment there was dead silence. Then an angry muttering arose. It swept like a wind through the council house. This was not Captain Wells! The angry voices grew louder. Why had Wells not come himself? It was an insult!

It was Shane who stood before them, not Wells. Wells had refused to come, just as Tecumseh had refused to go. He had written a letter instead, putting the President's message into his own words and sending it in his place.

---

[1] chiefs

11 ▲

Shane waited. He bore the crowd's anger bravely, knowing well the contempt they would have for him if he lost his nerve. At last Tecumseh spoke to his brother, who lifted his hand. The indignant crowd grew quiet, and at a nod from the Prophet, Shane began to read Wells's letter.

"Brothers," he began, "the Great Chief of the Seventeen Fires[2] loves his red children. . . ."

Stony silence greeted this announcement. Reading on, Shane reminded them how much the President cared about them and how carefully he protected their lands from his "white children." His audience was not impressed. The white chiefs always began their talks with flattering words and false assurances. It meant nothing. Sooner or later he would get to the point.

And he did. Just as the President would not allow settlers on the Indians' land, Shane read, "neither can he suffer his red children to come on the lands of the United States." Those living at Greenville were trespassing on government land. They must therefore "move from that place and off the land of the United States."

---

[2] the seventeen states of the Union

Shane sat down amid an uneasy silence. Tecumseh rose to his feet in a single fluid motion. Only his eyes betrayed the anger he was feeling. So this was what Wells wanted—to tell them to get off the land! Tecumseh swept his burning gaze across the faces turned to him.

Brothers, he began. Brothers! His voice became urgent. Time after time, white people have come onto Indian lands and taken them for their own. Jamestown was first. Plymouth next. The list goes on and on. Each time they sign a treaty promising to take only a little land, only the land they need. Each time they promise to leave the rest of the land for all to hunt on, as the Great Spirit intended it. Each time they break this promise!

Where are the Wampanoag Indians now? Where are the Narragansetts, the Pequots? Gone! Killed and driven from their lands by a people without honor, a people so greedy they must take all for themselves and leave nothing for anyone else. And now we are being ordered to move by the government of these people, as if their government, and not the Great Spirit, had created the land and everything on it.

"These lands are ours!" Tecumseh declared defiantly. "No one has the right to remove us because we were the first owners. The Great Spirit above has appointed this place for us to light our fires and here we will remain. As to boundaries," he said, "the Great Spirit above knows no boundaries, nor will his red people acknowledge any."

Tecumseh paused. Then, turning to Shane, he declared that he would have nothing more to do with Captain Wells. If the President had anything more to say to him, "he must send a man of note."

2 Two Brothers

Tecumseh had just finished speaking when a shrill voice broke in.

"Why does not the government send the greatest man they have to us?"

It was the Prophet, rising heavily to his feet. "I can talk to him," he said, with unmistakable conceit. "I can bring darkness between him and me. Nay, more—I can bring the sun under my feet, and what white man can do this?"

The Prophet looked about as if daring someone to answer, but no one did, and so the council was brought to an end. With an inward sigh of relief, Shane made his exit.

 16

The council house emptied out quickly after that. No one much felt like going back to work. The tribesmen were too fired up by Tecumseh's words. Even though he hadn't spoken of war, he'd roused the warrior in them with his bold talk.

It wasn't the first time. Tecumseh had learned to lead, to inspire his men, to take them on raids and bring them back alive. He had faithfully followed the path he had chosen so long ago, the warrior's path. But he had had help along the way.

His oldest sister, Tecumpease, had helped. When their mother left, she lavished her love on Tecumseh and became like a second mother to him. His oldest brother, Chiksika, guided Tecumseh like a father. He recited tales of Shawnee history and made Tecumseh repeat them over and over until he knew them perfectly. Chiksika took his brother hunting and taught him all the ways of the Shawnee warrior. Tecumseh was an eager pupil. His favorite games were war games. In pretend battles with his friends, Tecumseh was always the leader. The enemy, always the Long Knives.

When he became a warrior, though, he ran from his first real battle. He was fifteen, and

Chiksika had taken him along on a raid against a party of Kentuckians. At the first round of shots, Chiksika fell wounded. Tecumseh, suddenly terrified, turned and fled.

No one ever spoke of what had happened. The seasoned warriors must have understood about the first time, how courage can fail from inexperience. But Tecumseh was in an agony of shame. He vowed to himself to make up for it.

A few months later, Tecumseh was with another party of Shawnee braves when they ambushed some flatboats on the Ohio River. This time he attacked in the front rank, leaving behind some of the oldest and bravest warriors of the group. When the smoke cleared, all the boats were theirs and everyone aboard was killed. Everyone except one white boatman. And then Tecumseh's pride and satisfaction at killing cleanly in battle turned to shame and disgust. For the Shawnees, as was their custom, proceeded to bind their prisoner to a stake, pile dry sticks about his feet, and burn him to death.

Tecumseh watched silently. It was the first time he had ever seen a prisoner burned. When it was over, something in him snapped. He flew into a passion at the injustice of what they had done. It wasn't worthy of warriors, he cried, to

torture a helpless prisoner. Tecumseh was young, no more than sixteen, but he forgot he was lecturing his elders. He was driven to such eloquence that every brave present made a vow to give up this custom of their tribe. Tecumseh earned their respect that day. It would only grow as the years passed.

▲ ▲ ▲

The Prophet's beginnings were less promising. His life took a strange route before he came to lead at Tecumseh's side.

He was the youngest, born Lalawathika. Trailing along behind Tecumseh and the other children, Lalawathika was a lonely, awkward child. No good at games, not very popular, he was usually left out of things. Chiksika didn't seem to know he existed, and even gentle Tecumpease ignored him.

As he got older, he tried to get attention with loud, boastful talk (*Lalawathika* means "Noisemaker"), but no one listened. He picked fights with people to get them to notice him. He married and had children but was such a poor hunter that he couldn't feed his family. On top of it all—or maybe because of it all—he turned to drink. By the age of thirty, Lalawathika was a notorious drunkard and braggart.

Tecumseh was by that time chief of the village. He couldn't help being disgusted with his brother, but he pitied him, too. He supplied Lalawathika's family with meat. In the fall, when he helped the old people repair their wigwams, he helped his brother's wife repair theirs. He saw to it that the villagers put up with Lalawathika, if only out of respect for their chief.

Then a change came over Lalawathika. He fell into a trance one night in 1805, and when he awoke, he claimed to have had a miraculous vision. It was a vision of the future, he said, sent by the Great Spirit. The village was stunned. Lalawathika—a holy man?! Tecumseh went to see for himself and found his brother changed. The Great Spirit had sent him a vision, Lalawathika told Tecumseh. Now his path, too, was clear.

And so Lalawathika became a prophet. He stopped drinking and changed his name to *Tenskwatawa,* or "Open Door," because he believed that he would be the gateway to salvation for his people. He and Tecumseh started a new village together, at Greenville, where he began preaching. First Shawnees, then other Indians, began to listen.

Abandon the ways of white people, Tenskwatawa preached, for they are the children of the Evil Spirit. Return to the old ways. Live in peace with your neighbors. Stop quarreling among yourselves. Game is scarce and many are poor, but what little you have you must share. Other Indians aren't your enemy, he told them. They haven't fed you whiskey and taken your land and made you poor. The Long Knives have done this. They were made by the Evil Spirit to lead you astray.

So turn away from white people. Return to the ways of our ancestors. Give up the poison, whiskey. Defend yourselves with rifles if you must, but hunt with bow and arrow. Give up soft white bread and woven cloth. Wear buckskin and eat corn and wild game.

All this and more did the Prophet tell his listeners. He revealed new dances that the Great Spirit had shown him in his visions. He instructed them in new sacred rituals. And he held out a powerful promise: when all these things are done, he said, the Great Spirit will destroy the white race and give the land back to us as it was in the beginning.

▲ 22

It was a vision that seemed to promise an end to all the Indians' misery. As word of the new religion spread, pilgrims began to arrive in Greenville. Bands of Potawatomîs, Chippewas, Ottawas, Wyandots, and Delawares came from the north and west. They listened eagerly to the Prophet's talk. Some went back to their villages to spread the word. Others stayed on.

It must have been a heady time for the Prophet. For the first time in his life, people were listening to him. But for all his success as a preacher, the Prophet didn't know the first thing about running a village. With all the new arrivals, there was never enough food to go around. New wigwams needed to be built. Disease ravaged the village, killing some and driving others away. All these problems fell on Tecumseh's shoulders.

And the Prophet himself created problems. It seemed there was still a good deal of the boastful loudmouth left in him. Pretty soon he started to accuse people who refused to follow his teachings of being witches. In one Delaware village, four "witches" were burned alive by the Prophet's followers.

Tecumseh was outraged when he found out, and the witch-hunts were stopped—but not before the white governor of Indiana Territory had heard about them. William Henry Harrison was his name, and the Delaware villages were in *his* territory. He fired off an angry message to the Delawares.

"Who is this pretended prophet who dares to speak in the name of the Great Creator?" he thundered. "If he really is a prophet, ask of him to cause the sun to stand still—the moon to alter its course—the rivers to cease to flow—or the dead to rise from their graves. If he does these things, you may then believe that he has been sent from God."

Poor Governor Harrison. He was usually a shrewd man, but this time he blundered. He had completely forgotten about an eclipse that was due in two months. He'd even given permission to some scientists to set up observation posts in the territory. But the Prophet was shrewd, too. Somehow he knew about the eclipse. Fine, he said. He would perform a miracle. On June 16, he would send *Mukutaaweethee Keesohtoa*— "the dreaded Black Sun"—at midday.

He kept his word. On June 16, 1806, a huge crowd gathered at Greenville. They watched, terrified, as the noon sun grew dark in the sky. Then, seemingly at the Prophet's command, the

Black Sun grew bright again. From that day forward, no one dared challenge the Prophet's medicine—at least not within earshot of his followers.

So the Prophet's following grew, and in spite of his brother's faults, Tecumseh encouraged it. He may not have had any faith in his brother's sacred powers, but many other Indians did. They believed in his prophecies. They took a new pride in being Indian people. This faith and pride was bringing people of many different tribes together at Greenville. Tecumseh saw this, and in his mind an idea took shape.

He pictured Indians from different tribes— not just two or three tribes but all the tribes from Florida to Canada—standing as one against the Long Knives. He saw them united, refusing to give up their land, refusing to sign any more treaties.

It had never happened before. Indian people had never been one nation. They were divided into many nations, and those divisions ran deep. No one had ever been able to unite them. Even the great Pontiac had tried and failed. Maybe it was impossible. But Tecumseh was certain it was the only way his people would survive.

So he let the Prophet draw the crowds. He listened to his brother brag about being a great man and bringing the sun under his feet, and he kept still. For Tecumseh had his own vision of the future. It wasn't going to come true by magic or prayers or rituals. It wasn't that kind of vision. His was a warrior's vision, a statesman's vision. Tecumseh's time was coming, and he knew it. But not even he knew how soon.

3 The Voice of Bad Birds

After the council ended, Shane had hastily mounted his horse and set off for Fort Wayne to bring Wells Tecumseh's answer. The stars were out by the time he got there. Shane saw the lights of the fort first, like candles in the distance. Soon snatches of sound—laughter, a barking dog, a jingling harness—reached his ears on the night breeze. As he approached the stockade, he called out to the guard and the gate was dragged back. With a shake of the reins, he trotted into Fort Wayne, a United States military outpost in what was still, in 1807, Indian land.

Shane knew Wells would be angry when he heard Tecumseh's answer to his letter, and he was right. Wells was truly alarmed at what was going on at Greenville. All spring, bands of Indians had passed Fort Wayne on their way there. Supposedly they were pilgrims going to hear that Shawnee medicine man, the one they called the Prophet, preach his new religion. Maybe so, thought Wells. He'd seen families on the way to Greenville, not just warriors. But he didn't believe it. All those Indians gathering in one place made him nervous.

Wells had been stewing about the problem, and he thought he had it figured out. He believed the Prophet was planning a war against the white settlements. He thought so, first of all, because the Indians were so secretive whenever he tried to learn what their new religion was all about. Now why should it be a secret, he wondered, unless they were planning something bad?

Wells had also been listening to rumors. One rumor had it that war belts were being passed among the tribes from the Gulf of Mexico all the way to the Great Lakes, carried by Shawnee messengers. Another rumor said that the British up in Canada were giving the Indians guns and ammunition. Wells believed it. He wouldn't trust a British Indian agent as far as he could throw him. If the Prophet was planning a war, Wells would bet the British were behind it.

So William Wells had done his duty. He passed those rumors along. He wrote to people he thought should know about the threat brewing at Greenville. He wrote to the Governor of Ohio. He wrote to Governor Harrison over in Indiana Territory. He even took it upon himself to write to the secretary of war in Washington. To all of them he confided his suspicions about the Prophet. Then, finally, the President himself had answered, ordering the Indians to leave Greenville and go back to their tribes. But what good had it done? Absolutely none.

Wells wasn't the only one who mistrusted the Prophet. Most white people in the territory, and a lot of Indians, did, too. All the old, established chiefs thought the Prophet was an upstart and a troublemaker. Governor Harrison agreed, but he, like Wells, was convinced the British were telling the Prophet what to do. From what he'd heard of the Prophet, he didn't think the man had the brains or originality to stir up trouble on so large a scale. In his opinion, the

Prophet was "an engine set to work by the British for some bad purpose."

Shane's unsuccessful mission to Greenville did nothing to quiet the rumors. In fact, in the months that followed, they got worse. Wells sent two spies to Greenville, and they came back with wild reports. The Prophet was holding secret war councils. He was promising his people that the Great Spirit would destroy every white person in America. Every man in the village carried a war club.

Wells duly passed this information along, and the pressure on the Indians to leave Greenville mounted. The Ohio state government, the federal government, the neighboring tribes— everybody wanted them gone.

Governor Harrison finally sent the Shawnee head men a stern message. "My children," he wrote, "this business must be stopped. I will no longer suffer it. You have called in a number of men from the most distant tribes to listen to a fool who speaks not the words of the Great Spirit but those of the devil, and of the British agents."

Maybe Harrison was still smarting over his mistake about the eclipse. In any case, the Prophet didn't take offense. He sent a polite reply. The governor must have "listened to the voice of bad birds," he said. All that about planning an attack and working for the British—none of it was true. It was just a rumor.

▲ ▲ ▲

In the spring of 1808, one year after Tecumseh had declared that they would remain where the Great Spirit had put them, the Shawnees left Greenville. They gathered their few belongings, burned their wigwams, and set off for the headwaters of the Mississinewa River. There they built canoes to take them down the Mississinewa to the Wabash, and then down the Wabash to where the Tippecanoe River empties into it. On that spot they began building a new village, called Prophetstown.

It was a smart move. It landed them about one hundred miles farther west, which meant that the tribes visiting from the west had a shorter distance to travel. The forests that far west still held some wild game, and the rivers abounded with fish. Best of all, the Shawnee no longer had to live on government land, surrounded by Long Knives and enemies. Prophetstown was on Indian land.

It was also in Governor Harrison's territory—practically in his backyard. So he kept an even sharper eye on Prophetstown. He employed scouts and spies and traders to feed him information.

Of the Prophet's brother, Harrison heard nothing. Tecumseh hadn't spent much time at home after moving to Prophetstown. First, he journeyed to Canada to meet with British officials. They were quite impressed with him, and there was talk of a possible alliance. Then, he began his travels among the tribes, trying to persuade them to join a united Indian nation. In a single year, he met with Wyandots, Senecas, Sacs, Foxes, and Winnebagos.

Look at the fate of the eastern tribes, he told them. Do you think your fate will be any different? We must draw the line now! We must make ourselves so strong that the Long Knives will not dare cross it. If they try, we must put them back. And the only way to do that, he said, is to unite. Back in Prophetstown, the Prophet kept on preaching, but he was beginning to sound like Tecumseh. Mixed in with his prayers and sermons were calls for unity and demands for an end to land treaties. The new tone of his speeches alarmed Harrison even more. So when

the Prophet unexpectedly offered to come see him in person and put his mind at ease, he agreed.

The Prophet visited Harrison twice at his home in Vincennes, the capital of Indiana Territory. The first time, in August 1808, he brought a band of his followers. For two weeks straight he held religious meetings right under Harrison's nose. He ranted and raved, but only about the evils of alcohol and war. By the time the Prophet left Vincennes, Harrison had decided that maybe he wasn't so bad after all.

But for the second visit, the following year, Harrison was on his guard. By that time his spies had brought him a lot more suspicious information. He'd heard of a failed plot among the Great Lakes tribes and the British to attack American settlements. When he asked the Prophet what he knew about it, the Prophet replied that of course he'd advised against it. It went completely against his principles.

That's fine, Harrison told him drily, but then why didn't you inform me? Surely you must have known such a plot would interest me.

The Prophet was at a loss for an answer.

"I must confess," Harrison wrote later, "that my suspicions of his guilt have been rather

35 ◢◣

strengthened than diminished[3] in every interview I have had with him since his arrival." There was no doubt left in Harrison's mind. The bad birds were right. The Prophet was dangerous. Somehow he must be stopped.

---

[3]weakened

▲ 36

4 The Fort Wayne Council

In July of 1809, something happened to take Governor Harrison's mind off the Prophet and his plans. He received an important letter from the secretary of war, a letter he'd been hoping to get for a long time. The letter gave him permission to go ahead and negotiate a new land treaty with the Indian nations.

Harrison was delighted. Nothing would please him more than for Indiana to become the eighteenth state of the Union. But a territory couldn't apply for statehood until it had sixty thousand free white citizens. Now, in 1809, most of Indiana Territory still belonged to the Indians. Their land was off-limits to white settlers—although whites crossed over and tried to settle on it anyway, which naturally made the Indians fighting mad. The part of Indiana that did belong to the government was gradually filling with settlers. But there still weren't enough to apply for statehood.

A nice, fat purchase of some of that Indian land was the only way Harrison knew to get rid of the Indians and attract more white settlers. That was where the treaty came in. As Tecumseh had rightly said, white governments had been making treaties with Indian tribes since the very beginning. A treaty was like a contract. According to the contract, one or more tribes agreed to give land to the government in return for money, goods, and the promise that the rest of the land would remain theirs forever.

A treaty set a boundary between the Indians' land and the government's land. It was supposed to be permanent. But each time the government wanted more land, it proposed a new treaty with a new boundary. Little by little, treaty by treaty, the Indians lost their land.

Now they were about to lose some more. Harrison had his eye on about three million acres of land. He'd made treaties before—lots of them—so he knew how to go about it. First, he contacted a handful of his closest friends among the chiefs, offering them bribes in advance to agree to the treaty. Then he sent word to the tribes: a great council was to be held at Fort Wayne in September. For weeks Harrison's runners pounded the traces from village to village, inviting chiefs and warriors of many nations.

All the tribes of the Miami nation were invited, of course. They had lived along the Wabash and its tributaries for generations. Plus, they were loyal friends of the United States.

The Delawares were invited. They were recent arrivals, having been pushed, over the years from the Atlantic Coast to Pennsylvania, from Pennsylvania to Ohio, and then from Ohio to Indiana. Harrison knew there was discontent among the younger Delawares. But the village chiefs were his friends. He didn't think they would object to giving up their land one more time—if the price was right.

The Potawatomis were invited. They lived far to the north of the lands Harrison wanted. They only roamed south to hunt once in a while. But Harrison asked them to come anyway. He said he didn't want anyone to accuse him of not including an interested tribe. The truth was that the Potawatomis were wretchedly poor. Harrison felt sure they could be persuaded to give up land they hardly used in exchange for money and goods.

Some tribes should have been invited but weren't. The Shawnees at Prophetstown had as much of a claim to the land as the Potawatomis. But the Prophet and his brother definitely *weren't* invited. Harrison wanted only agreeable chiefs at his treaty council, not chiefs who would make trouble.

The Kickapoos should have been invited because they lived on part of the land Harrison wanted, but they weren't invited, either. Harrison had the idea that if he met with the Kickapoos later and showed them a treaty already signed by all the other tribes, they would be more likely to agree to it. So that's what he did.

You see, Harrison thought of himself as quite an expert on Indians. "Savages," he called them—but not to their faces. To their faces he called them "my children." He believed they were trusting, but not trustworthy; clever in their own way, but certainly no match for him; courageous in battle, no one would deny, but they didn't fight by the rules. All of Harrison's opinions were like that—based on white ideas of the way people should be. So of course even the "best" Indians didn't quite measure up.

After thirty-five years of living on the frontier, Harrison thought he knew all there was to know about Indians. So he was confident as he rose to speak to the chiefs that gathered for the Fort Wayne treaty council in September. He was a tall man with long legs, a long face, and a long thick nose. He towered over them as they sat in the traditional circle.

They were mostly old men, their brown faces lined, their shoulders a bit stooped. Some of them had been great warriors in their younger days. But now they were "government" chiefs, village chiefs who had long ago given up the dream of driving back the Long Knives. Game had grown scarce, their villages were poor, and their children's bellies were often empty. They depended on the money they received every year under earlier treaties.

For eight days, Harrison and the chiefs negotiated. Around and around they went. They took turns making long speeches in the council house. They talked about it in the evening over a whiskey cask in the governor's tent. The chiefs discussed it in private councils and the tribes-

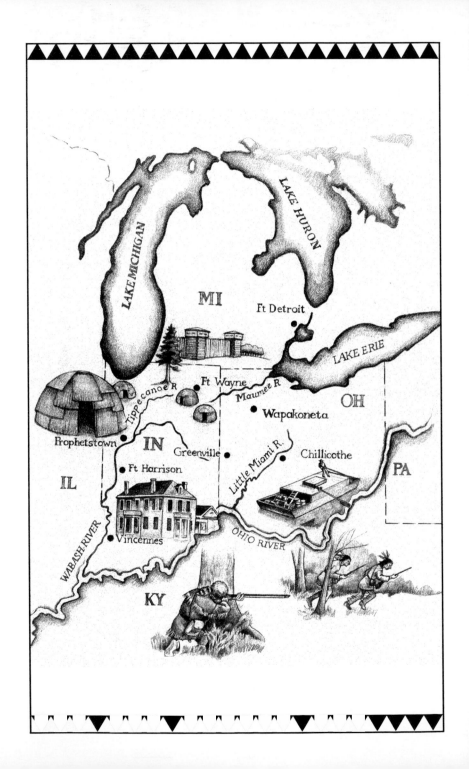

LAKE MICHIGAN

LAKE HURON

MI

Ft Detroit

LAKE ERIE

OH

Tippecanoe R.

Ft Wayne

Maumee R.

Wapakoneta

Prophetstown

IN

Greenville

Little Miami R.

Chillicothe

PA

IL

Ft Harrison

Vincennes

OHIO RIVER

WABASH RIVER

KY

men discussed it in their wigwams. The tribes disagreed among themselves, and once a fight almost broke out. The Miamis, of all people, took the most convincing—and they were usually the most agreeable of the gathered tribes.

All in all, it was a lot harder than Harrison had thought it would be to get the chiefs' agreement. But he succeeded in the end. He appealed to their pride, to their greed, to their very real need, and to their friendship for him. Finally, on the last day of September 1809, the chiefs put their marks to the Treaty of Fort Wayne in the presence of 1,392 of their tribesmen. Harrison had scored another victory. The Indians had lost another three million acres of land.

5 Prophetstown

Not long after the Fort Wayne Council ended, the weather turned cold. Bitter winds tore through the trees, stripping leaves from the branches and dancing them ruthlessly about. Under a leaden sky, the air smelled of snow.

At Prophetstown, Tecumseh sat in his wigwam, staring moodily into the fire. He was thinking about the Fort Wayne Treaty, going over and over it in his head. He'd been sitting here when the runner had first brought the news. He had listened, and when he understood what had happened, his handsome face twisted with fury. They must die! The chiefs who signed the treaty must die! He called an emergency council to announce the news. Before a council house filled with warriors, Tecumseh and the Prophet both vowed to kill the chiefs who had betrayed them.

The Fort Wayne Treaty seemed to have caught Tecumseh by surprise. He'd been away most of that summer, visiting the Sacs and Foxes who lived along the Mississippi River. In village after village, warriors shouted in angry agreement when he called on them to join him in standing against the Long Knives. By the time he got back in August, it was too late to stop the Fort Wayne Council from taking place.

So he'd sent spies to the council to keep him informed of what went on. He flushed with anger all over again thinking about it. He knew those old village chiefs were weak and corrupt. But the younger ones, the warriors—why had they gone along with it? He'd counted on them to stop the treaty from going through. But no—more than a thousand warriors had all just watched their chiefs sign away their land forever! Couldn't they see that this was the road to destruction?

Tecumseh watched the flames dance. Winter had set in. There wasn't much he could do about the treaty right now except council and plan and store up his anger. He'd learned a hard lesson. He'd discovered that his following among the tribes was not yet as strong as he'd hoped. But that would change, he thought grimly. Come spring that would change. It was time for him to make his move, to step out of the shadow of his foolish brother. He jumped up, and, yanking the door flap to one side, he stalked out of the wigwam into the freezing air.

▲ ▲ ▲

Spring that year—1810—was glorious along the Tippecanoe. On its fertile riverbank, the women of Prophetstown were planting corn. They stooped and dug and sowed the corn, talking and laughing as they worked. Each woman said a prayer as she planted—that the corn should grow tall and the harvest once again be bountiful. For the number of visitors to Prophetstown was growing, and all needed to eat.

Just that spring hundreds more had arrived. Warriors mostly—Potawatomis and Kickapoos, with some of the younger Miamis and Delawares. Angry about the new treaty, they were ready now to join Tecumseh. At the end of May, more than 240 Sacs and Foxes had arrived from western Illinois. They had set out from their villages as soon as the grass was tall enough to feed their horses. What they saw as they rode in may have surprised these warriors from the plains. Instead of the usual clusters, the bark wigwams of Prophetstown covered the slope up from the river in neat, orderly rows. There were six hundred of them. The traditional council house stood on the outskirts. Nearby stood the Prophet's medicine lodge. Within, it was said, the Prophet received his holy visions from the Master of Life.

But these warriors hadn't come to hear the Prophet speak of holy visions. They had come at the calling of Tecumseh.

Tecumseh was busy that spring. In May he visited Wapakoneta, a village of Shawnees led by a rival chief named Black Hoof. Black Hoof was a government chief. He had long been one of the brothers' bitterest foes. His people lived in log houses, tilled the soil, and raised cattle and pigs. With their white ways, they were exactly the sort of Indians the Prophet and Tecumseh had always condemned.

Still, the Shawnees at Wapakoneta were Tecumseh's kinsmen. He decided to make one last try at persuading them to join him. Perhaps this new treaty would open their eyes.

Not surprisingly, Black Hoof and his chiefs refused to meet with Tecumseh. But a crowd of younger Shawnees gathered, curious to hear this chief their fathers called a renegade. And at first, to their ears, his talk was wild indeed.

War, Tecumseh told them, was now certain. Listen, before it's too late. Don't trust the Long Knives! They are deceiving you. They do not care about you.

Suddenly there was a commotion in the crowd. A big man came forward, waving a piece of paper. Tecumseh recognized him. It was Stephen Ruddell, a white man who'd been captured and adopted by the Shawnees as a boy. He and Tecumseh had been close friends once, but not any longer. Ruddell had gone back to his own people and become a Christian minister. He was at Wapakoneta as a missionary, teaching the Shawnees to live like white people.

Ruddell walked toward Tecumseh, holding the paper high in the air. You're mistaken, he told Tecumseh firmly in Shawnee. The President in Washington does care about his Indian children. Here is a letter from Governor Harrison to prove it.

Ruddell shook the paper out, as if he meant to read it aloud. Before he could utter a word, Tecumseh was by his side in a few long strides. He snatched the paper out of Ruddell's hands and flung it into the fire. If Governor Harrison were here, he said, I would do the same to him!

Turning his back on Ruddell, Tecumseh faced the young Shawnee warriors. Come back with me! he urged. Come, stand against the Long Knives! The tribes on the Mississippi have already joined, Tecumseh told them, and he would not rest until all the tribes were united. Even if I am to die, he declared, my cause will not die with me. An excited murmur ran through Tecumseh's young audience. Here was a true Shawnee! A brave, independent spirit, not like their village chiefs, whose council was always to wait, to be patient, to give in. Tecumseh's talk was fiery, yes, but it wasn't crazy. It made sense! One after the other, in firm, excited voices, the young men gave their pledges to join Tecumseh at Prophetstown in the fall.

The next day Tecumseh rode out of Wapakoneta with the most eager recruits by his side. He arrived home in high spirits, only to find the village overflowing with visitors, the Kickapoos upset, and his brother in a mess.

49 ▲

It seemed that while Tecumseh was away, the government had sent a boat up the Wabash to deliver salt to some of the tribes that had signed the Fort Wayne Treaty. The salt was part of their payment. The captain landed at Prophetstown, thinking he would deliver the Kickapoos' salt there, since so many were now living there. But the Kickapoos angrily opposed the Fort Wayne Treaty and refused to accept the salt. The Prophet couldn't make up his mind what to do. Finally he told the boat crew just to leave the salt on the riverbank until his brother got back.

They did and continued on up the Wabash. On their way back downstream, they stopped again at Prophetstown to find out about the salt. By that time, Tecumseh was back. He made up his mind quick as lightning. Grabbing the boat captain, he ordered him roughly to take the salt back on board. Never would he accept payment for this treaty! The boatmen did as he said and went on their way, frightened but unharmed.

▲ ▲ ▲

It was high summer now, and the forests around Prophetstown seemed to deepen and grow quiet in the heat. The corn brushed against the women's legs as they walked between the rows. Even with all the warriors and their councils, a lazy peace seemed to settle over the village. Then, on a fine afternoon in July, a messenger from Governor Harrison came trotting into the village.

The governor, it seemed, had kept himself informed. His spies, two French traders, had told him about the hundreds of new arrivals and how angry they were over the Fort Wayne Treaty. Harrison had heard all about the burning of the letter and the refusal of the salt. It seemed to prove what he'd suspected all along: the Indians were preparing for an attack. So he'd sent his white translator, Joseph Barron, with a message.

Barron dismounted and was brought to stand before the Prophet. The holy man sat surrounded by Indians of different tribes. Barron could read extreme displeasure in his face. With his good eye the Prophet glared at Barron for several minutes in cold silence.

"For what purpose do you come here?" he finally spat out. "Brouillette was here; he was a spy. Dubois was here; he was a spy. Now you have come." His voice became deadly. "You, too, are a spy." Pointing to the ground at Barron's feet, he cried, "There is your grave. Look on it!"

The Prophet's men moved toward him menacingly. At that moment, the flap of a lodge door was pulled aside and Tecumseh stepped out. Instantly the Prophet's men grew still. Without looking at his brother, Tecumseh walked to Barron and greeted him coldly. Your life is in no danger, he told the nervous Barron. What business brings you here?

Barron then read Harrison's message to the assembled warriors. In it he warned the Prophet of the folly of making war on the United States. "Do not deceive yourself," it said, "do not believe that all the Indians united are able to resist the force of the 17 fires even for a Moon. I know your Warriors are brave, ours are not less so, but what can a few brave Warriors do against the innumerable Warriors of the 17 fires?"

Harrison's message challenged them to prove that the chiefs who had signed the Fort Wayne Treaty had no right to do so. And with the warning and the challenge, Harrison sent an invitation. The Prophet could, if he wished, take three chiefs and travel to Washington to a council with the Great Father himself. Harrison would arrange it.

A flicker of surprise passed over the faces before him. This was unexpected. Barron was told he must wait for an answer. The council fire burned late that night in Prophetstown. When it went out, a decision had been made. This time Tecumseh, not the Prophet, would go to Vincennes and meet with Governor Harrison. He would answer the Governor's challenge in person, with his warriors by his side.

6 Meeting at Vincennes

Barron had much to tell upon his return to Vincennes. He'd spent the night in Tecumseh's lodge and the two had sat up half the night talking. Tecumseh had denied any desire to make war. But he'd also "declared most solemnly" to Barron that the Indian nations could not remain at peace with the United States unless the government gave up the idea of settling more land to the north and west.

It was the first time Harrison realized who Tecumseh was. Before that he was merely "the Prophet's brother."

"This brother," he now wrote, "is really the efficient man—the Moses of the family . . . described by all as a bold, active, sensible man, daring in the extreme and capable of any undertaking."

When Harrison learned that Tecumseh was coming with his warriors, he immediately sent a runner to Prophetstown to tell him not to bring too many—a dozen at most.

He needn't have bothered. On August 12, a procession of eighty canoes came gliding down the Wabash River. They were brimming with crimson-painted Shawnee warriors. At Fort Knox, just three miles from Vincennes, they were stopped by a Captain Floyd. "I examined their canoes," he later wrote, "and found them well prepared for war, in case of an attack. They were headed by the brother of the Prophet (Tecumseh), who, perhaps, is one of the finest looking men I ever saw—about six feet high, straight, with large, fine features, and altogether a daring, bold looking fellow."

At Harrison's fine brick mansion, everything was ready for Tecumseh's arrival. Benches and chairs were set out on the large covered porch overlooking a grove of trees. An honor guard from Fort Knox was present, in full-dress uniform. A Potawatomi government chief named Winimac was there. And at the governor's invitation, an audience of officials, judges, and distinguished ladies and gentlemen was gathered on the porch, all chattering expectantly.

Suddenly someone caught sight of Tecumseh approaching through the grove. The excited babble of voices fell to a whisper. He strode toward them, followed by thirty hand-picked warriors. Clad in buckskin and brilliantly painted, they held tomahawks and war clubs at their sides. In silence they came, holding themselves ramrod straight and proudly aloof.

The Shawnees halted within several yards of the house, and Barron went to ask them to join the others on the porch. Tecumseh declined. He preferred to hold council where he now stood, under the trees.

But there are no seats here, Barron said. Indians have no need of seats, Tecumseh replied. Only your seats need to be moved.

"Your father requests you to sit by his side," Barron persisted, and anger flashed across Tecumseh's face.

"My father!" he said, jabbing his finger toward the sky. "The Great Spirit is my father! The earth is my mother—and on her bosom I will recline." He sat abruptly, and his warriors promptly sat down behind him. Harrison had no choice but to have all the seats moved to the grove.

The council that thus began under the trees lasted on and off for ten days. Though surrounded by Long Knives, Tecumseh spoke fearlessly. He admitted that he and his brother were organizing the tribes to stop further advances by the whites—what else could they do? They had been driven almost into the Great Lakes by this new treaty.

The land belongs to *all* the tribes, said Tecumseh heatedly. It is common property, not the property of a few chiefs or tribes. The government has no right to decide that this strip of land belongs to the Miamis, that to the Delawares, and so forth. The Great Spirit gave the land to all his Indian children to use. It cannot be sold without the agreement of everyone. *He* had not agreed to sell the Fort Wayne Treaty lands, nor had his people. Only a few chiefs had agreed to it. And those chiefs, Tecumseh said, looking at Winimac with hatred, would be executed.

A nervous murmur ran through the crowd. Winimac, who was sitting in the grass near Harrison, pulled out a pistol and began to load it. Harrison began to explain that the United

States government always tried to be fair to the Indian people, but before he could finish Tecumseh leaped to his feet.

"Liar!" he roared in Shawnee. He poured out a stream of angry words, and an army officer who understood Shawnee ordered his soldiers forward. Tecumseh's warriors jumped up and raised their tomahawks and war clubs. Harrison drew his sword, Captain Floyd drew a knife, the men in the audience grabbed for their weapons, and the troops cocked their rifles.

For a long moment, no one moved. Then Harrison ordered the soldiers to lower their rifles. Declaring the council at an end, he turned on his heel and walked into the house.

▲ ▲ ▲

The next morning, when Tecumseh's temper had cooled, he sent the governor an apology, which Harrison accepted. They talked a great deal more before the council was through, but neither side budged.

Harrison refused to give back any of the land acquired by the Fort Wayne Treaty. He claimed that the treaty had been negotiated fairly. Tecumseh insisted that it hadn't been and that the land still belonged to the Indians. If the government tried to have it surveyed, he warned, bloodshed would result. And if the land wasn't returned, the chiefs who had signed the treaty would be killed and he, Harrison, "will have a hand in killing them." The old government chiefs no longer spoke for the people, Tecumseh said. The warriors were running things now, and he was their chief. "I am alone the acknowledged head of all the Indians," he said.

How then, Harrison interrupted, would the tribes receive their yearly payments? Usually the money and goods were given to the village chiefs to distribute.

"Brother," Tecumseh said, "when you speak to me of annuities,[4] I look at the land and pity the women and children. I am authorized to say that they will not receive them, Brother. They want to save that piece of land. We do not wish you to take it. It is small enough for our purposes. If you do take it, you must blame yourself as the cause of trouble between us and the tribes who sold it to you. I want the present boundary line to continue. Should you cross it, I assure you it will be productive of bad consequences."

---

[4] yearly payments

▲ 60

Lastly, Tecumseh said that until their plan to unite the tribes was complete, neither he nor his brother would accept Harrison's invitation to go to Washington. But, he added sadly, he hoped the Great Spirit would tell the President not to demand the lands. The President, he said, "is so far off he will not be injured by the war. He may sit still in his town and drink his wine, while you and I will have to fight it out."

The council came to an end. That afternoon Tecumseh and his warriors left for Prophetstown.

7 Trouble Coming

The weeks passed, summer turned to fall, and the fighting Tecumseh predicted didn't come to pass. On the surface, everything was peaceful. But there was a feeling of uneasiness in the autumn air, as distinct as the tang of wood smoke in the wind. Everybody started making sure which side everybody else was on, just in case. Things stayed that way during the winter. Heavy snows and bitter cold kept people at home, gathered around their fires. In Prophetstown snow drifted deep around the wigwams, but everyone inside was warm and well fed. The Great Spirit had been generous and had sent a bountiful corn harvest. The British had been generous, too. Tecumseh had gone to Canada again that fall, to ask the British for help. The British Indian agent there had sent a pack train with supplies. So no one at Prophetstown went hungry.

Then spring came, and the tension that had been lurking beneath the surface sprang to life. Reports came of Potawatomi and Kickapoo raids on white settlements in Illinois. All along the Kaskaskia and Big Muddy rivers, settlers abandoned their homesteads. From the Fort Wayne Treaty lands came the news that one of the Miami tribes—the Weas—had frightened off the surveyors who'd begun surveying the land. The Weas hadn't hurt them, just scared them half to death, but it was a bad sign, Harrison thought. Very bad. The Weas were usually the most peaceful of tribes. Tecumseh's influence must be growing.

And indeed it was. In June, Tecumseh traveled to western Michigan to recruit more Potawatomis and Ottawas. He sent messengers across the Mississippi River to meet with the Iowas and to Ontario, Canada, to talk to the Mohawks. While he was away, the Prophet ordered his men to seize a boatload of salt that was on its way up the Wabash. They would be needing it, he told the captain boastfully, when his brother returned from the lakes with two thousand warriors.

Two thousand warriors! That clinched it for Harrison. He'd heard that the Indians at Prophetstown were planning to attack him at Vincennes, but he hadn't believed it. The Prophet could never pull it off. "Nothing but the great talents of Tecumseh," wrote Harrison, could hold together the motley collection of Indians at Prophetstown. But Tecumseh with two thousand Potawatomis and Ottawas under his command was a different story. (The Prophet was exaggerating, as usual, but Harrison didn't realize it.) This was a force to be reckoned with.

Harrison wrote immediately to the secretary of war and asked for army troops. He issued an order forbidding gunsmiths and merchants to sell ammunition to the Prophetstown villagers or to repair their rifles. And he sent his most menacing message yet to Prophetstown.

"Brothers," he wrote, "the tribes on the Mississippi have sent me word that you intend to murder me and then to commence a war upon our people . . . you are about to undertake a very rash act; as a friend I advise you to consider well of it . . . do you really think that the handful of warriors you have about you are able to contend with the power of the Seventeen Fires . . . ?" The Long Knives are "as numerous as the mosquitoes on the shores of the Wabash. Brothers," he warned, "take care of their stings."

Back from Michigan, Tecumseh was puzzled by Harrison's message. Planning his murder? What a ridiculous idea! That would get them nowhere. Tecumseh was preparing to defend Indian land. He'd admitted as much. But as long as the Long Knives stayed on their own side of the treaty boundary, they had nothing to fear. Harrison obviously didn't trust him.

Tecumseh knew he had to be careful. He wanted to frighten the Long Knives into keeping off the Indians' land, but he didn't want to frighten them into starting a war. Not yet, anyway. And not at all if he could help it. The warrior in him would have been only too happy to fight, but Tecumseh wasn't just a warrior. He was a chief, a statesman. He had to think of all his people—the old men, the women, the children as well as the fighters. He would rather use the threat of war, not war itself, to keep the Long Knives back.

If it came to a fight, then so be it. He wasn't afraid to raise the tomahawk. But it was still too soon. He had brought the northern tribes into his confederacy, but he still had to go south. He needed the Creeks, the Cherokees, the Chickasaws, and the Choctaws. Then he'd be ready to stop Harrison.

So Tecumseh sent a brief reply, promising to visit. He tried to calm Harrison's fears. "I hope that when we come together, all these bad tales will be settled; by this I hope your young men, women, and children will be easy. I wish you, brother, to let them know when I come to Vincennes and see you, all will be settled in peace and happiness."

▲ ▲ ▲

The mood at Vincennes when Tecumseh arrived in July of 1811 was anything but peaceful and happy. Harrison didn't believe for a minute that Tecumseh was coming to make peace. Tecumseh was an Indian, and Harrison didn't trust Indians. He actually thought Tecumseh might try something during his visit. So he called out the militia, and eight hundred men from the countryside answered the call. The garrison at Fort Knox was alerted, and soldiers were stationed in Vincennes. Their orders: to patrol the streets day and night.

By the time the council began, the air was thick with tension and mistrust. Harrison, backed up this time by hundreds of soldiers, took a lordly attitude with Tecumseh. He refused to discuss the Fort Wayne Treaty, saying that it was now in the hands of the President. He demanded an explanation for the seizing of the salt. And he told Tecumseh that if he really wanted to show friendship, he could turn in the two Potawatomis who had murdered four settlers in a raid that spring. They were believed to be hiding at Prophetstown.

Tecumseh was too smart to let himself get ruffled by Harrison's high-handed manner. Angry words and threats wouldn't work this time. He dismissed his brother's actions as being of no importance. Last year you were angry that we refused the salt, he told Harrison. Now you are angry that we took it. Perhaps, he said with a trace of a smile, it is impossible to please you.

As to the murders, Tecumseh was very sorry for them. He admitted the murderers might be followers of his, but he didn't know where they were hiding. They weren't at Prophetstown.

▲ 68

Tecumseh was really only interested in one thing: his plans for uniting the tribes. He spoke quite openly. It had been difficult, he said, but at last he had succeeded in bringing the northern tribes together under his leadership.

Now why, he wondered, is this so alarming? He was only following the example of the United States, which had formed a strong bond between its fires to defend itself against an enemy. He was uniting the tribes for the same reason. But Indian and white people don't have to be enemies, he said. If the Long Knives would respect the boundary between their lands, they could live side by side in peace. This was what he wished.

At the close of this council, he announced, he was setting off for the southern tribes to get them to join, too. He asked that everything stay as it was until he returned. For his part, he would send messengers far and wide to keep his followers from doing any more mischief. The government, he said, must keep settlers off the Fort Wayne Treaty lands. When he got back, he would go to Washington and settle everything with the President.

Harrison's answer was short and unpleasant. The moon, he declared, "would sooner fall to the earth than the President would suffer his people to be murdered with impunity[5] . . . he would put his warriors in petticoats sooner than he would give up a country which he had fairly acquired from the rightful owners."

Harrison then broke up the meeting. It was the last time Tecumseh would ever talk of peace with the Long Knives.

---

[5] without punishment

8 | Tippecanoe

With Tecumseh and his warriors gone, Harrison lost no time writing to the secretary of war about the council. He was struck by how easygoing Tecumseh had seemed. "To have heard him," Harrison wrote, "one would have supposed that he came here for the purpose of complimenting me."

But Harrison mistook the war chief's reason. He thought he'd scared Tecumseh into being agreeable. It was "the gleaming and clanging of arms" that did it, "the frowns of a considerable body of hunting-shirt men, which accidentally lined a road by which he approached to the Council House." If Harrison thought Tecumseh could be cowed by dirty looks from a bunch of Long Knives, he was wrong. Tecumseh was biding his time.

It wasn't that Harrison didn't respect Tecumseh. He did. He called Tecumseh "one of those uncommon geniuses, which spring up occasionally to produce revolutions and overturn the established order of things.

"If it were not for the vicinity of the United States," Harrison wrote, "he would perhaps be the founder of an empire that would rival in glory that of Mexico or Peru. No difficulties deter him . . . For four years he has been in constant motion. You see him today on the Wabash and in a short time you hear of him on the shores of Lake Erie or Michigan, or on the banks of the Mississippi, and wherever he goes he makes an impression favorable to his purposes.

"He is now upon the last round to put a finishing stroke to his work," continued Harrison. "There is no doubt but his object is to excite the Southern Indians to war against us."

But was Harrison worried? Far from it. "I do not think there is any danger of any further hostility until he returns," he wrote. Actually, this was his big chance. With Tecumseh out of the way, only the Prophet remained—and he lacked "judgment, talents, and firmness." Harrison had been wanting to squash him for a long time. Now he would kill two birds with one stone. He would march an army to Prophetstown, dispose of the Prophet, and crush the confederacy in one move.

▲ ▲ ▲

Two months later, Governor Harrison—now General Harrison—once again sat busily writing to the secretary of war in his large, loopy hand.

> Camp on the Wabash
> 65 miles from Vincennes
> October 6th, 1811

Sir:

> I have the honor to inform you of the arrival of the troops under my command at this place on the 2nd Inst.[6] The regular troops stood the march surprisingly well. . . I have reconnoitered[7] this country nearly to the boundary line and have fixed upon this as the most eligible situation for a fort. The timber is now preparing and it will be finished with all possible dispatch. We have as yet seen no Indians. . . .

---

[6] of this month
[7] explored

From inside his canvas tent, Harrison only half heard the shouts and grunts and ringing of axes as the men put up the stockade. His mind was elsewhere. More than anything he wanted to get to Prophetstown. But Harrison was a soldier, and soldiers obey orders. His orders were to build a stockade first. Then his orders were to try to crush the Prophet's following without bloodshed. If he must engage in battle, his orders were to win.

So here they were, cutting down trees instead of fighting. It was true they hadn't seen any Indians, but Harrison was sure the Indians had seen them. Sure enough, before the week was out, a sentinel on night watch was surprised by an Indian who reared up from the bushes, shot him in both thighs, and melted back into the darkness. An alarm was raised and the troops turned out to scour the woods, but they found no one.

Harrison could hardly contain himself. Why, this was no less than a declaration of war! "I had always supposed that the Prophet was a rash and presumptuous man," he wrote, "but he has exceeded my expectations." Still, orders were orders. He asked a group of friendly Delawares to visit the Prophet and warn his people to lay down their arms and return to their tribes, or face the consequences. "They were badly received," wrote Harrison, "ill treated and insulted and finally dismissed with the most contemptuous remarks upon them and us."

What's more, the warrior who had shot his sentinel returned to Prophetstown while the Delawares were there. He and the small war party with him were among the Prophet's closest friends. There was no doubt now that the Prophet had taken up the tomahawk against the United States. "Nothing now remains but to chastise him," Harrison wrote, "and he shall certainly get it."

On October 29, Harrison rode out of the stockade at the head of nine hundred men. Their destination: Prophetstown.

▲ ▲ ▲

The night was cold and a light drizzle misted the air, but inside the medicine lodge it was warm and smoky. The Prophet sat alone, motionless. Since Tecumseh left he had been spending more and more time here, strengthen-

ing his medicine and talking with the Great Spirit.

He had promised his brother that he would be cautious. He had promised to do nothing rash or provoking. But how could he heed his brother when the Great Spirit's voice was so loud in his ears? *He* was in charge now, not Tecumseh. He'd sent that war party to shoot at the Long Knives on purpose, to bring them on. It had worked. They would be here before the sun set twice more.

And look at how he'd thrown those Delawares out of the village with jeers and threats ringing in their ears! He couldn't resist sending them off with a boast: he would burn the first four Americans taken prisoner.

The Great Spirit was leading Harrison right into his hands. He was sure of it. It had happened once before, with the eclipse. Now it was happening again. The Prophet prayed more fervently than ever for guidance. The war dances went on day and night.

▲ ▲ ▲

On the afternoon of November 6, 1811, the Prophet's scouts burst into his medicine lodge with news. The Long Knives were here! Hundreds of them, marching out of the woods just a mile west of the village. They'd march right into Prophetstown if they weren't stopped. The Prophet, roused from his trance, did the first thing that came into his head. He sent three warriors with a flag of truce to tell Harrison that he didn't want to fight. He would gladly meet with Harrison the next day to try to settle their differences peacefully.

Harrison's officers were all, to a man, against a truce and in favor of attacking immediately. But their orders were to avoid bloodshed if possible. So Harrison agreed to a truce until they could meet the next day. His officers grumbled, but they did as they were told. They made camp within sight of the village, on a stretch of high ground dotted with bare oak trees. The soldiers pitched their tents, built bonfires, and proceeded to cook supper and hang up their wet socks and breeches and long johns to dry. As evening drew on, the order came down: all troops were to sleep in battle formation, clothes and boots on, weapons by their sides. Harrison wasn't taking any chances.

Less than a mile away, the Prophet sat before

the fire in the council house, surrounded by leaping, chanting, red-painted warriors. His single eye gleamed with excitement. A necklace of deer hooves rattled on his chest, and his hands nervously fingered a string of holy beans. Tonight was the night. Tonight the Master of Life would give him medicine to bring his warriors a great victory. Tonight he would make rain and hail to wet the Long Knives' gunpowder. He would send confusion among the Americans, put them into a trance and make them stupid. His warriors would be invincible. But they must attack tonight. And they must kill Harrison.

At a little after four o'clock the next morning, Harrison had just awakened and was moving about his tent. Outside in the darkness, the cooks were feeding the dying fires and preparing to cook breakfast. In a minute or two, the bugle would blow to rouse the men.

Just then the sharp crack of a rifle echoed through the silent camp. In every tent eyes jerked open, hands flew to rifles, blankets were thrown off. Harrison hurriedly stuck his feet into his boots and shouted for his horse. A second shot rang out, and then the war cry exploded from the attackers' throats, high and shrill and piercing as arrows. The battle had begun.

The first attackers had surprised a sentry, who'd fired off a shot and gone running back into camp. The warriors pursued him right into the camp, killing a handful of soldiers as they emerged, wild-eyed, from their tents. Some soldiers scattered, but most managed to form ranks even while being shot at, taking cover behind tents, trees, and bushes. Soon the Indians were attacking from all sides, their aim deadly in the light from the bonfires. The soldiers gave it back, firing into the darkness from their lines. Over the din could be heard Harrison's voice, ordering reinforcements wherever the attack was heaviest.

For two hours the battle raged. Finally, in the dim gray light of dawn, the Indians could see that the American lines were still holding. One by one, they began to slip away. Harrison ordered a final bayonet charge that sent the remaining warriors fleeing back to their village. The battle was over. The Long Knives had won.

9 Tecumseh's Return

It was a weary band of travelers that rode out of the leafless forest that cold January day in 1812. Their horses were thin and walked with their heads down. As they started across the snow-covered plain, the icy wind whipped their faces and stung their eyes. The riders clutched their blankets closer. They were almost there.

At the head of this little band rode Tecumseh, returning with his followers to what was once Prophetstown. Now it was nothing but a heap of cold, dead ashes. They reached the village outskirts and paused. There were the charred remains of the council house, sticking up through the snow. They walked their horses down a smooth, snowy slope where rows of wigwams once stood. No one said much. Finally, at a word from Tecumseh, they urged their horses on, eastward. He'd seen enough.

Tecumseh's tour of the southern tribes had failed. The handful of Creek warriors who rode with him now were all he could persuade to join him. He'd done his best. He'd been on the move for six months. He'd smoked the pipe of peace at one council fire after another, with Creeks, Choctaws, Chickasaws, and Osages. He'd spoken to great crowds of warriors, spoken brilliantly and passionately. He'd spoken the truth. But no one believed it.

Tecumseh was sure—as sure as he was of anything—that the Indian tribes could only survive if they united. Separately, they were doomed. Of this he was certain. But he simply couldn't convince the southern tribes. They'd been enemies of the northern tribes for so long they just couldn't change. And some, like the Cherokees, had adopted white ways. They trusted the white government. Fools, thought Tecumseh bitterly. Just wait until the Long Knives decide they want your land. Then you'll see what the government's promises are made of.

Tecumseh was in southeastern Missouri when the news reached him of his people's defeat on the Tippecanoe. But nothing prepared him for the destruction he found when he got to Prophetstown. The entire village was burned to the ground. Even the corn harvest, five thousand bushels hidden in the forest, had been found and burned by Harrison's soldiers.

Tecumseh and his men rode on, to a camp nearby where the Prophet was living with a few Shawnees and Wyandots. They spotted the smoke rising through the trees from the few wigwams clustered pitifully together. So many painful feelings must have been churning inside Tecumseh as he dismounted before his brother's wigwam—anger and rage, sadness and frustration. But he held himself with dignity. He was not defeated yet.

Tecumseh ducked to enter the wigwam. Inside, several figures sat wrapped in blankets around a fire. His gaze slowly traveled over them and lighted on his brother, huddled on the other side of the fire. Tecumseh's look seemed to command his brother to stand up, for when the

Prophet met his eyes, he slowly got to his feet. No one said anything.

The Prophet trembled to see his brother look at him so. He'd seen that look before, like the eyes of a bull buffalo before it charges.

The day of the battle had been awful for the Prophet. The warriors had crowded in on him, accusing and blaming him for their defeat. He'd tried to explain, tried to tell them he would bring victory the next time, but they threatened him with death and he shut up.

But this was worse. This was Tecumseh. He knew he should speak, but he didn't know what to say. So he kept quiet.

Finally Tecumseh spoke. He didn't shout— not at first. He almost whispered, and that sinister whisper was more terrible than any shout.

Lalawathika, he hissed. You disobeyed my commands! This was not part of my plan, to shed blood at this place! Fool! On and on he went, blaming the Prophet for letting Harrison draw him into battle, for sending his warriors into a disaster.

But it was words, only words, and the Prophet must have been relieved. He must have felt safe. Because, true to his name, he opened his mouth. He tried to make excuses.

But the Long Knives were here, he started to say. My medicine failed because—

Silence!!

It was almost a scream. Tecumseh flew to his brother's side and grabbed his hair with both fists. He tugged fiercely and the Prophet's eye closed in pain. I'll kill you!! If you ever get in my way again, I'll kill you!! Tecumseh seethed with anger. He shook the Prophet by the hair again and again and again. His voice reached to the heavens. You have destroyed everything! Now I have to start over! I have to start all over because of *you*!

Tecumseh gave the Prophet's limp form one last shake. Then he flung his brother away from him and walked out.

Epilogue

▲▲▲

Those two hours of desperate fighting before dawn on November 7, 1811, went down in history as the Battle of Tippecanoe. It wasn't a big battle, but it was an important one. Like a pebble thrown into a pond, it made a small splash, but the ripples seemed to go on and on.

The secretary of war, writing to congratulate Harrison on his victory, called it "a conflict unparalleled in our history." He meant that there had never been a battle like it before. He was wrong, of course. American Indians and whites had fought before, and they would again, many times. Harrison, however, was quite proud of himself.

The fact that Harrison had taken his army onto Indian land and provoked a fight didn't seem to bother many people. His supporters cheered and nicknamed him "Old Tippecanoe."

Many years later, when he ran for president with a running mate named Tyler, their campaign slogan was "Tippecanoe and Tyler too!" Harrison won that election and became the ninth President of the United States.

The Battle of Tippecanoe was the end of Tenskwatawa's career as a prophet. He eventually moved west to Kansas, where he died in 1837.

For Tecumseh, the Battle of Tippecanoe was a terrible setback. The Prophetstown Indians scattered far and wide after the battle. Most went back to their tribes. Some rode west and took their revenge on the white settlements there. Many who had followed Tecumseh now turned their backs on him.

But true to his word, Tecumseh started over. Slowly he gathered his scattered warriors together. In June 1812, as he was working to rebuild his confederation, the United States declared war on Great Britain. It was a war that had been brewing for a long time, and Tecumseh knew what he'd do when it came. He led his warriors to Canada and joined the British side. His genius as a war chief guided the British in their most important victory of the war: the capture of Detroit.

On October 5, 1813, Tecumseh was killed on the field of battle fighting an American army led by his old enemy, Harrison. It was a battle that almost didn't get fought. The British general was afraid to take on the larger American force. He'd been retreating for days and wanted to keep on, but Tecumseh shamed him into making a stand. The odds were against them, but Tecumseh wanted to die fighting, not running. On the morning of his last battle, he seemed almost happy. "Father," he reassured the frightened general, "tell your young men to be firm, and all will be well." But all was not well that day. Tecumseh was killed.

Tecumseh had been right about so many things. But he was wrong that day at Wapakoneta when he said that his cause would live on after him. With Tecumseh's death, his followers grew discouraged and the movement to unite the Indian tribes ended. Individual tribes continued to fight for their lands. As white settlement spread across the continent, alliances between tribes were formed to resist it. But the dream of a single Indian nation was gone forever. It died with the dreamer.

Afterword

This story has been written almost two hundred years after the events in it took place. It is as accurate as any story can be two hundred years after the fact. Some descriptive details were made up, but only to bring the people and events of the story to life—not to alter them.

Some speeches and bits of conversation appear in quotation marks, while others do not. The difference is this: some of the things people said were remembered and written down word for word in letters or journals. When such accounts were available, they were quoted. Oftentimes, however, the things people said were remembered in a more general way. When that happened, the exact words of a speech or conversation had to be made up. They were not presented in quotation marks.

Notes

Page 1 The first white frontiersmen who ventured from Virginia into Kentucky and Ohio were called "Long Knives" by the people there because of their long hunting knives. The name soon came to mean all white American frontiersmen.

Page 4 Information about what went on inside the council house during the raid on Black Fish's village comes from Joe Jackson, a white captive who was in Chillicothe at the time. The Long Knives named the attack "Bowman's Raid." Jackson is quoted by Bil Gilbert in his book *God Gave Us This Country*.

Page 6 Tecumseh is not mentioned specifically in accounts of the Long Knives' attack on Black Fish's village, but as a leading boy in the village and Black Fish's adopted son, it is unlikely that he would have failed to take part in the village's defense.

Pages 8–15 Shane himself recounted these incidents in an interview in 1821. His comments are found in the Tecumseh Papers of the Draper Manuscripts, which are kept by the State Historical Society of Wisconsin.

Page 11 The Prophet accidentally shot himself in the eye with an arrow when he was about 17.

Pages 14–15 No text of this speech remains except for the quote on page 14, which Shane recalled from memory several years after the fact. Shane described Tecumseh's speech as an "impassioned and glowing harangue of considerable length on the injuries by the whites and their encroachments on the lands of the red men. . . ." The quote and description are from the Draper Manuscripts.

According to whites who heard Tecumseh speak in later years, Tecumseh had an impressive command of the history of tribal-white treaty relations. He never failed to give his white audiences a history lesson when he spoke. Tecumseh made it a point always to speak publicly in Shawnee, so any texts of his speeches that were written down are translations.

Pages 17–20 Details about Tecumseh's childhood come from Shane and Stephen Ruddell. Ruddell, whose Shawnee name was Big Fish, claimed to be a particularly close friend of Tecumseh's as a boy.

Page 28 Fort Wayne was on a small piece of land that the tribes, as part of a treaty, agreed to let the United States government use. Such small tracts of government land within Indian territory were called "reservations."

Pages 31–32 Harrison was a prolific letter writer all his life. When his house burned down in 1858, most of Harrison's personal papers and many official documents were destroyed. Luckily, a large volume of correspondence remains. This is the source of the Harrison quotes, the speeches from Tecumseh and the Prophet to Harrison, and of Tecumseh's speeches at Vincennes.

Pages 37–43 This account of the Fort Wayne Treaty Council is based on an official journal kept by Harrison's secretary. Some history books say that Harrison got the chiefs drunk and then put the treaty in front of them to sign when they didn't know what they were doing. That doesn't seem to have been the case here, although Harrison did bribe and manipulate them. However, Harrison, who by this time had acquired almost thirty million acres of tribal land for the government, was notorious for using such tactics in other treaty councils.

Page 43 Miami, Delaware, and Potawatomi people were, of course, no more greedy than anyone else. Their government chiefs, however, were in a position to profit from treaties, and sometimes they let greed get the better of them. Treaties usually said that the yearly payments were made to the chiefs, who then handed out shares to the villagers. This gave a chief the chance to keep what he wanted for himself or his family, and also boosted his importance among the villagers. Of course, Harrison knew this, which was how he got certain chiefs to sign away the land.

Pages 44–46 Although there is no record of Tecumseh sitting and brooding in his wigwam on any particular day, I took the liberty of putting him there to show his point of view about the treaty. Everything that goes through his mind is based on fact. It is known that Tecumseh was in the village that winter, that he did call a council and threaten the chiefs' lives, that he was terribly angry, that he had sent spies to the council, and so forth.

Pages 48–49 This account of the burning of Harrison's letter comes from a letter from John Johnson,

Indian agent, to Harrison. Johnson had heard about it from the chiefs at Wapakoneta and from Ruddell. The description of the young Shawnees' reactions is based on the journal of a Major John Norton, a half-Cherokee and half-Englishman who visited Wapakoneta just days after Tecumseh had departed. His friends at Wapakoneta reported that Tecumseh "had persuaded the greater part of the people of this village to join him at the Wabache. . . ."

Pages 52–54 Barron himself recounted the incident described in these pages.

Pages 56–57 Captain Floyd wrote about Tecumseh's arrival in a letter home a few days after the event.

Page 57 Different versions of this exchange between Tecumseh and Barron exist in different sources. Mine is based on the one in Glenn Tucker's *Tecumseh, Vision of Glory*.

Pages 73–75 This description of Harrison's march to Prophetstown is based on his own numerous letters to the secretary of war.

Pages 75–77 All sources say that the Prophet was spending a great deal of time in his medicine lodge during this period, so I have put him there in order to show his point of view.

Pages 78–79 These details of the Prophet the night before the battle come from David Edmunds's *The Shawnee Prophet*.

Pages 79–80 This is based on several accounts of the battle given later by United States Army officers.

Pages 83–86 What happened between Tecumseh and the Prophet in this scene was never recorded word for word. But Shane said that Tecumseh was "prevented with difficulty" from killing his brother, that he grabbed him by the hair and threatened his life. Shane's recollections are found in the Draper Manuscripts.

Kate Connell lives in New York where she works as a writer and editor. Ms. Connell is also the author of *Tales from the Underground Railroad* and *They Shall Be Heard.*